John Garvey

ENCOUNTERS

Also by Daniel Berrigan

Time Without Number
(1957 LAMONT POETRY AWARD)

The Bride: Essays in the Church

DANIEL BERRIGAN

Encounters

Published by The World Publishing Company

110 East 59th Street, New York, New York 10022

Published simultaneously in Canada by

Nelson, Foster & Scott Ltd.

Library of Congress catalog card number: 60-5806

Second printing—October 1971

Grateful acknowledgment is hereby made to *Poetry Magazine, The Commonweal, America, Thought,* and *Spirit* for permission to reprint poems which first appeared in those magazines.

WORLD PUBLISHING

TIMES MIRROR

In omnibus quaerant Deum.
–Ignatius Loyola

For those who love all things.

Contents

PART 1

PART 2

Part I

Eve

It was for love of me
Adam undid Christ. And I must encounter
of my sour body that sole golden fruit
Mary; and say to her

how rope-ends of his scourging
aeons long, we wove and grasped firm:
how thorns we grew, our first tears'
harvest for his crown.

Woman to woman's heart
I will go. Miles are years from Eden to that hill
but I will take for sign, if so she know me
blood on my face

where I cried out and buried
my lips in Abel's murder. I will follow
the unhealed scar the tree Christ dragged
opens in time

unto her side. The poor go
for comfort to the poor. Because she wears
his holy blood, Abel's will start upon my tears
and cry her mercy.

Across years, across the stilled
hearts of our sons: drawing the vicious
thornbrake aside, sundering the serpentine rope
her hand reaches my own.

Abel

One blood veined us, stem and fruit
weighing our mother Eve. Brothers
said her burning eyes: see, hand
must lock in hand: five fingers root
in no rock than this other: Abel
in Cain, younger in his brother.

My mother, the worm that raveled Eden
tents in the parent tree.
                                        New lambs
sniff and shy at my blood: go red fleece
teach death to my mother.

Noe

Whispered to me: will you mount the waters?
while Lucifer rose serene, and noon sun showed
accustomed face

the ship stood
wooden, portentous, a hollow horse
the children climbed and garlanded for doom.
Good burghers I saw swimming to their eyes
in fishes' tears, or theirs: above hammer blows
while we ribbed heart in her, was it mockery
or drowning cries?

would know, we and they
day she hurried into element, great flanks
breathing a threnody, Jonas whale
hoisting the white bird, an only hope.

Abraham

To see my small son
running ahead: pausing above a flower,
bringing to me some trifle of hedgerow
wearying, sighing, seeking my hand

unable in all his being
to give death credence, when upon him
no death was, but only his heart agile
to prove youth upon a ditch or stile:

to see this you must know
my heart like kettledrums had commanded
alarms and marches, and shaken age
like treason from its majesty.

My heart stood now in breast
an underheel flower, and wilting
its last sun away that drummed
I am nearer I am death

Who is child now? who is old? my tears
or his song? I am sift of dust
in that Hand unmercifully blown
through mountain passes, a consummation

no nightmare of mine had groaned.

Love Me, His thunder never cried
in my worst dream. *Love me*
my child's eyes never cried
until this dawn, and under under my knife

Isaac

My heart slows to my father's
or to death
                    over stile and ditch
spends youth, over a landscape
my father's tears make me

my father if so the Father will
I draw knife
in your drawn hand for instrument

my father
when I walked frail as morrow
out of you
                    your blood stood
stern at my heart. Today it bids
like cannonade its will:

wear faggots like a savior:
of unstained thirsting stones
build me an altar: open
four wounds of awaited Christ.

Job

I stood sons up like shields, leather and bone
nudging time back. Warrior faces
burnished gold on hide, met his brute wrists
that swung fire on the tents.
                                        But my daughters
limbs marveled to bear
hands shaped of flowers. Of purpose I stood firm
lest you be shaken overmuch. Let no wind
forbade my prayer, no hail, no intemperate hour
strike. Who touches
in envious breath their name
                                        invades my breast
bears off its heart on pikestaff. My daughters

we shuffle to grave. Miserere unravels
fine clothing, bodies, to a spool of stuff.
Winds shake down
and go unpunished, you from autumn limbs.

Elias

Childhood I stumbled through, a sleepwalker
at dawn abed

no evidence upon him: did he crouch above pools
fishing his drowned image? not a sere leaf
fallen from boughs to eyes: none.
Chaste
as waterfall, hoarse as ravens: as before
but named man now.
A widow's tears
for only son, waxen and unexistent:

would I enter in? would I assuage her?

Image poured upon absence, child,
come back. Pulse to wrist, sight
welling in eyes, spiraling music in ear:

I held to heart
an old man's childhood, a ghost in tears:
why, why awake me?

Ezechiel

Forest cut off at youth's high tide
bloodlet, stripped of heyday and brought low

where is green crown you carried high, blue height
you married? deprived

of bird's throat, of Adam's cords whereof
brave music is plucked:

son of man, put forth My riddle.

Dark side of time woke to one dawn
a plain of uncreated men: skulls stood
like ripe fruit of an Eden tree
and sang like throats of birds clinging that tree:

once upon a death was victory

Christ

Words are outer form
wherein majesty might near, if so it please:
of limb and mein not substance,
but evangel light glancing, announcing: lo, he cometh.

Words summon her too, the mother, infolding
like a kerchief, odor and form of him who lay there:
so in repose her body grew
a spiritual space to round and radiate you:

your friends, whose memory
calls up your ghost at cockcrow: there and not there
if tears glister or no:

so, struck from your holy flesh, distance and
access, our words begin like lepers' bells: O come
not near.

Mary

Offer a time when Christ's mother's name
was green among his people, a great name
too near for legend. Such that a stir went up,
an indrawn breath among the old at fireside brooding:
while her youth is our own, no one can die.
We grow young too, peeking the son
she carries carefully as flowers: ah well-a-day
she sings him, my lovely one.

But evil the trees stood for her, evil the waters:
yet did the well mock her: *draw of me deep*
I will draw deep of you, in tears and doubly.

Yet did the trees stalk her by dream, and try
her light-latched heart for fear: *I will drink*
blood of your blood: I will bear high and proud as you
your lovely one, and ill-a-day it whispered.

Poems, like life, come to a dark mood.
I offer you waters and trees you love. Beware them.

Saint Ann

(who bore a daughter in late life)

Hand that folded and laid aside my fabric
as it pleased Him
                    when it pleased Him, shook me out,
billowed and filled me like a silken tent
pegged in mid-desert.
                    He struck eventual waters
from this worn stone.
                    A voice, I come
shaking the women up at dawn, barefoot
through burning snow, and shouting *manna manna*

Saint Joseph

I

One corner of field my plow veered from
as a prow, sailors tell, turns stubborn aside
shaking spray like a great *no* from mane
away from drowned men that aeons down
walk bones about and wave sad bells in hand.

was I harboring a curse afield? nothing so fierce.
it was mere shale turned the plowhead over.

yet in June month, year upon year
when fields were a broth of kitchen greens,
wheat and corn to knee—southfield

unplowed, unbidden, stood up like a summoned bride
and came toward me in roses.

It made a plowman wonder
to bring from fields
some Power beyond me had sweetened to garden—
flowers, armfuls of flowers, to her.

Saint Joseph

II

She would cross noon fields
bearing the child, into shadow
of trees that stood stock still, even in May wind.

waiting me, she settled into some task of women
as bows the head and sets the fingers flying,
a busy stillness at the heart.

about her tree, the plow blade that had moved
straight as a weapon against rock or root
relented, cut a corner, until one day

it was circle upon circle, close and closer
I wove a furrow about the still tree
and stiller Mary. Like earning and entering
paradise: from labor to mild joy, from action

to adoration.
                    At the still center she
and the child aimlessly gathering
wild grasses: into one hand, the scattered leaves gathering
of the universe.

Saint John Baptist

I

A sword forbade me to grow old: it cut
time like a parasite from eternity.
My angel, standing upon that arc, had laughed to see
Herod wield Excalibur: of double mind, and even now
sweating with unbribed dreams.

I stooped and touched my eyes
to peace. Womb, desert, dungeon, light and dark.

When first I heard His voice, I wakened
drowning in my mother. Holy waters, holy wastes
grew me, emaciate shadow

I am gone before Him
a few years, like His shadow. He must follow on
the way a man wills, and wills his shadow, one.

Could death have eyed and pierced my body, could I
for sign have stood upon the nails an hour,
would He take warning from His murdered shade
casting His fate to ground in smoky runes
with points of light like lips where death had fastened?

Love is no warning. I foot Him from sad limbo
till death unfasten, till His rising spring me
unwind and wear me—aureole, choir, and crown.

Saint John Baptist

II

In the mirror a sword made descending
briefer than image a stream carries
beyond, I saw John old: eyes cold, hair silver.

Look how I save you sang the blade strongly:
freedman: do not upbear on shoulder
dwarfing honors, prophecies by rote
a stalemate heart.
                                        I caught in two hands
this unripe storm-shaken fruit, by hate
(by love) tossed down. Held it for thanksgiving

to taste at soul's mouth its salt vigor.

Saint Magdalen

Two pebbles make marriage rings on water
but hairfall, fall of tears, require of no one:
will you take me?

I have sought the outlasting essence to give:
since joined hands join but skeletons, and I see
two skulls shed irony on each other's smiles
and diggers arrange the marriage bed.
                                                            Though death
artfully unweapon woman of all
words, veils, tears, heart's blood,
                                                perfume
fueled from generative flowers, murmurs its
spiritual, learned-by-heart soliloquy. Say for me

Magdalen's eternity is at your feet.

Lazarus

Sister, you placed my heart in its stone room
where no flowers curiously come, and sun's voice
rebuffed, hangs on the stones dumb. What I could not bear
I still must hear. Why do your tears fall?

why does their falling move Him, the friend, the
unsuspected lightning: that He walk our garden
with no flowers upon His friend, but a voice splitting
my stone to a dream gone, my sleep

to day? what, what do tears say to Him?

what did He say in tears, that His grief fall
scalding my hands, that cold hands sprung
sleep like a manacle, and drew my eyes a space
that had seen God, back to His human face?

Saint Peter

No Christ at a tombstone
knocked me awake. A cock mounted the tall
rock where His body bled. I choose
that rock to stand: man
and clean of hand and blessed, whose
even second choice was Christ.

Apostles

ringed Him about then,
not twelve profiles for a frieze
by artisan's hand scored, worried perfect:
Caesars, prophets, judges: would history have tossed
a rust coin on our future? doubt it.

No Moby, no conquistadors
but landmen groaning green on a two-mile pond
and He stepping dry-shod as a Red-Sea Jew
cradling
distempered night to a babe's closed eye.

we grew gentle to harbor
in Christ's dream of us
someday. Beached, and found
twelve dead men flung, wearing our faces drowned.

Saint Stephen

That day stones fell
I stood them to a cairn and died
unknowable, a mound of dust for heaven
to make man of.
                                        That day stones beat
like stone beasts for a forced entry
to eat my heart: I prayed awhile
then opened brief and tossed them meat.
They ate and died of it: unproofed against
my living phial, great love.
                                                  That day
stones flew like hail of stones at first:
my dolorous flesh took their brute will
in heavy sighing: but stones transformed
to tongues, whispered at every wound:
welcome.
                    That day stones flowered
to dark rose-field Christ walked and gathered.

Saint John of the Cross

let go days that are
runners in relay, a spent calendar

let go hours that went
song and composing throat, to element

let go hand that lay
in hand, long as a loved shade

lingeringly outstays its dream
to nether star   cock   the omni-seeming

sun. Let go works cunning and crude
that pled well for you, suing
respite: but Christ weighs them from rood

right hand and left: lets fall
man   breath   artifact   and all

save what nailed there
dying eyes light on and dress fair

Part 2

What We Name Permanent

Trees stand, individual bell-notes on air
holding as long as hearken, shape of the bell.

What we name permanent, tinkering with true order
is a smoke: eyes are their brief lightning,
voices drown in wells of voice: *gone gone* is all
they stay to say. Friend is gone, time rides the moon
to occupy his shape: winter, the egg of a worm, tents
upon spring: he will eat man to a standing shin.

Limb born of limb
as starpoint sprung from star:—only to fall from dark
its light made tolerable? No: I dare

write it. But trees decline to youth, flowers
spring their dry rot, glances gone
brim the socket into second sight.

Reaching To Quench a Light at Midnight

Perhaps light
is irrelevant, and mind shunts for a lifetime
about its metaphors, holding puffs of flame before
old runes,
                    when darkness alone
unseals the stern profiles of stone, and exhales
for man's trouble, for compassion, one authentic ghost.

In a dark wood, in dark waters: by terror
man drowns or mounts himself.
                                                    Then
out with the hoarded flame: call courage
transfiguring, that moves forward under no
torch's numen, to the dread presence

whose hand one's hand must grasp: a flower
(dark will not tell) plucked from hell or heaven?

Faces

Flower bears flower interminably.
Miles of them, light in dusk: no calling halt
the bride's procession toward the ghost bridegroom,
the invisible knifing prow
for want of sound, for dearth of shape, named time.

I marvel: as flower bears
  like an arrow: as though grown, feather for flower
  from heart's blood

as flower bears flower
  like a bird its plumage, wingbeat for voice
  hinting what eye, what mandarin heart
  this skillful fan conceals

look: face flowers in face too.
They rise, as toward one sun two blooms, toward one height
wings. Instructed? they are grown
from Eden and Easter ash, deep in time sown.

Like Very Men

How will you have stars? in you, your eyes
that lead others a chase merry and weary?
But fair weeps to unfair, eyes dim early.

Lucky the child stars light on, you say. Kings
undergo deserts to him, cheerfully shoulder
whole sacks of toys. But lucky the boy

is a silly word. Look the great planets
in eye, that spelled out brazen
happy birthday Christ: and were liars

seeing kings rode off his page and died easy:
while stars, or their degenerate sons, no comfort shed
but shied and hid, like very men, from that hillside.

Mosaic: Florence

Stones are life?
impossible they should warm, transmit blood,
be man.
                    But stand back:
with a great indrawn breath the countenance
creates itself. Hands cry: believe me.
Heart grows wakeful for responsibility.

Give life a space:
the violin runs
if it have hush for that fierce gantlet
straight on the massed brasses, dies
impaled and singing

Two Images in a Room

A mother blesses the Son
struck from her stone body:
crossways on her robe, a long vein mars
herself and Him: by lucky chance, makes lucid
the hammer notes like bell blows
late, but summoning her hour
and His:
                opposite, stone turns to Him.
I thirst? strike the rock
it will bleed, it is not we. Into one abeyance cast
bones of slain lamb
pestled in earth's earthen bowl
with tears of the arrowstruck hare.

Time gently composes
Christ, mother, artist, into this death.

The Dying of Eugenio Pacelli

Go bring me
while sight blunts to a cripple's thumb
the beggar at my posts, that we may whisper
deprivations.
          Have you seen Jesus Christ? he noosed me
with three keys like millstones, bade me founder
toward him upon the equinoctial fury.
                                 Come beggar or
Majesty, take my hand
                    that unslips as you hold it
                                    soul

But

Scarecrow vine decked out in the wind's
derision, tattered with seventy years'
hoe, clod, and harrow: who'd have thought
the old man's blood ran hot as pudding: in
bottles, muttered like genie for an out?

Old trees too, hidebound, embalmed, holy
India buries standing, kindles them round
to a pyre, till flames explode
last tear from eye or heart.
                                        Even this
ashy ritual and black bone is phoenix nest,
annunciation, May. Fruit like children's flesh
pushes into birth. Last breath is
newborn.
        Die? yes, but like this.

Vale

We look in friend's eyes:
a lightless withdrawal, a landscape
never again love will resume

and dare say:
memory uncages all of spring

go bring sight
bring voice to the blind magnificent trees

that by mere endurance are all but men

Chorale

as though time fitted them
masks of age
the very young do sleep.

tempering with blinds
sun from their faces
is a kindness—
                              but autumn light
brings down, as leaves in weather
shadow of leaves on them,
                                               as time on mortals
vapor of time on these slight ghosts.

Lend us the moon
that is not truth but seeming
more exquisite than the blunt eye of day
to all defenseless things.
                                                Bats newborn
misshapen children, moles,
innocent of every sin but ours
                                                            beseech
by lightless eyes, her falling light to them

Snowman

The children wrapped up and skeined out and
rolled downhill death, who is ludicrous

but king too, from coal eyes surveying
kingdom, from ruined mouth saying: *it is all like me:*

no blue or red of vein or knick-knack heart
fired and set afoot, I do permit me.

The dwarf at shoulder, looking out of eyes
secret and simian, I do dispense with.

But head to boot one element, one temperate
cold requiring.
                    His fallen coals weep and are granted:
spare me sight of the unlike world, its hearts and

heats and blueveined men

Hear Ever So Gently

Permanent beauty stands
nowhere under the tense
mainspring of time.

while I praise maiden-
color and -voice of flowers
stealing my heart aside

so frail they are, this night's
starlit air has felled them.

a gray cathedral takes
enemy year after year
deeper the spiritual thrust
on stained and wrinkled stone.

somewhere between its bones'
imperceptible wound
and the star-crossed flower

above a rust of bloom
under the doomed tower
hear: ever so gently

a main and springing hour

Vocation

Hemlocks in row, heads bowed beneath snowfall
like abstract old men, raven of hair once

but age is upon them: sorrow and reversal
in one night's course,
gently exhorted
into longsuffrance by winter birds: in moonrise,
twilight, inching their shadow onward.
Eternity
is eventual: through time, the trail is sparse and
wavering: a star's flare, a wounded bird in snow:

vocation a ghost's cry: *which way is man?*

Recollection

I love aftermath of action: the mind's
courteous attendance on memory of sound.
So a whole sea coils and sleeps in
a shell inspread: the ear
fills with voices that recede farewell,
harkens lost voices larger back.

Violin
unskeins its floating spiral, raises
and lowers footfall upon it. *Who goes there?*
Leave it unanswered. If you love, if you
hardly can bear, there is no other.

An Old Woman in Death

For *words words* death's instantaneous
waterfall granted all at once
what sun fumbles weeks upon, and only debatedly
brings to pass: I say spring

that springs her absent eyes:
like flowers whose seed dies in
temperate air, they fade here: but in height
elsewhere, are majestic blue

blue wept her eyes when she cried aloud:
in fear or exaltation, no man
can translate. But woman who died
shook a worn garment aside

bride somewhere again by loving makes beautiful.

Tree: October

under that summer cloud
whose rain is red and gold

around that vase's cunning
figures whom storm and calm
scatter to make again

about that summering swan
whose plumage winter hastens
away
        beneath those bells
whose beat broods on the air:

music, plumage, rain
whatever image hung

the great tree at heart

is fled   is flown   is spent.
skeleton: element

I Sing Memory

that clothes
air with trees, trees with dawn, birds with
no net or death plummeting down. Celebrate

sudden transparencies in a loud room, hearts
reddening a colorless world. Sing

icy boughs warming, sun more earnestly
bent to wheel. Praise steady sorrowful eye

summoning angels to ring and befriend
man's bootless sorrow.
But will have man
austere, aware, strung, threatens the unsheathed
shadow, I remember, of San Angelo's sword.

Man Is More

than a face his father yearned
over still waters. Behind that irony
carved and enclosed, soul
is personal diamond: into dark says:
stars are more than dark refuses them.

Man is more than day denies him:
all things of stone or music, setting against time
a living shoulder, a flower's stubborn
delicacy.
Soul is a soul changed
in mid-journey to nightingale:
it sits the golden bough, unreels its voice
far even as us: I am wronged
but not silenced: I pour my light, my coals
upon just and guilty. Bear it
who can.

The dancer improvises and is hardly there:
a whirling diamond: each attitude
a universe. Our hearts cry
sensing through ease that agony: be still.
One could as well halt the heart cold.
No: he must mime life to life again.

Not invisible, but strictly contained. You must
keep vigil, not be above

lowly unexpected showings. I see him
in shape of hand, cleave and bid aside
the dark. Or with password *friend* pass
in another's eyes. Suspect tenderness
of harboring him.

Meeting Over the White Flowers

Love to believe a bowl of white flowers
is the universe. Stars measure
from its tranquillity, their exiles:

an inviolate Cathay floats gently in its truth:
we dare venture only into seas breathing to us
like our own name, odors that start tears,
we must not ask why.
                                        Men and women
never think to mourn, meeting over the white
flowers: *we are outside, alas, one tower of bloom
is not Eden.*
                              But until evening, no asp stings.
Believe the vanished bird that dwelt them sings.

Men Were the Image

Unlike a fish that gestures feebly
with waving fronds from far back in time
I am still unborn
                                        or a bat, blind
Icarus aground, limping in harness along:

trees confound death
by uprightness: they answer violence like a
gospel man:
                              when storm made evident its brute will
and we, not falling to knee, rued dearly

men were the image: in calm a dance gesture,
in sorrow, joy. We shook night from limb
and stood: an arched instrument loud with them.

A Statue of the Blessed Virgin, Carved in Wood

Wood is noble when it forgets to resemble

and like the first idea of tree
stands straight up and awaits creation.

Then art is arbitrary; and by exquisite
tricks of trade, hairfall and sandal and maidenhand,

decrees what moment Mary will pause in. Forbidding
lips their sound, shapes a phrase
of universal mercy. And the delicate outthrust foot
protests and starts: you are my errand.

Atlas

Roots curled fastidious,
a fern at window
eyes the great-boned maple steadying for death. A cat
sat at a bullfight, and was bored.

Samson's falling takes time
down with it: a week, a month, paid
in precious blood stains the earth gold. Dying,

he shelters the bewildered driven flocks:
greatness wears its lionheart and
fleece. He will never say it: autumn's
shouldered burden pales and crumples
manifestoes of summer love. Atlas
take up the cross.

Love Is a Difference

Water is the shaping form whose dull weapon
molds and heats
fish to jeweled finish. You never saw
men more at home, or out of native air
so soon lost.
                    Love is a difference: I thrive
on death to you. But man lends reason to,
whispers *here and now* to
                                        air cut to his profile:

as a bell lifts throat to pour on four
winds their christening: or majestic birds, daring
a perilous clearing, teach light its spectrum.

Beethoven's Violin

(for Carol and Jerry)

Birnam Wood across the plain, marches
season after season, into itself. When
morning searches a voice, takes voice,
only another day, yes. But the first astounding day of all
dawns from that throat.

Tenderness and strength
do not dwell in one life. Yet the violin
summons tears and commands action.
Its best face is the smile
on face of Christ: at end
it calls halt triumphantly, pouring best wine last
upon task done: it is achieved, sings

fearfully and wonderfully made, sings
the violin. I have taken wings at morning
I have searched the uttermost sea: there is no one
to love me like this lover. I am Eve, sings the violin:
I am taken from his side: I heal with my body,
with sounds his hands make on me
the wound I opened him.

Domes

                        that raise the improbable to an art,
buttresses momentary and airy as a
wing studied for the space of its alighting

shadow:
                the chief ingredient of victory is
defeat. Unless life remain supreme
huts and wattles are the swinish

address of man. Someone must be born to say
I had rather written such a line and
died without signing it, than borne home to my empress

encircled Moscow's sword.
                                        Who says it?
no reward is commensurate. But confer on him
in springtime, the procession winding toward Chartres

or Rouault's Christ, mourning upon his city.

More Like the Sea

(A man is more than two sticks crossed.
He is more like the sea, bringing up God knows what
at any moment: Conrad.)

Nail him to sticks
he stands free and makes sense
even of agony, even of sticks and stones.
No grafting him on: his fruits
are free, and other: more men loved,
more years' intensities. He ranges and rejoices
the horizon sorrow lifts him to.

Look how hands refuse
all but their own gift. That blood will flow
red red against bitter
hemlock, maple sweet. Blood writes
what heart provides: God knows what
that sea brings up.

God bring that sea safe
—safe is no word for him—but a
surf home, shuddering its coast
crying hoarse in its falling
victory.

Radical Strength

issues in marvels:

shoulder and thigh follow through: one
crucial delicate finger at the flute stop.

Hill eases itself like tiger's body, around one
blind tuft of violets.

A spring after, felled oak has one
heartbeat unspent: one
handful of leaves in a dead hand.

Child Above a Flower

                                        unsure
if he regards
or is regarded.
                        Both is a truth
older will fade.
Come, said flower
race me to evening.
                                Time is a way
no one knows.
                        Who
goes there?
                    who went there
answer man's tears, sighs

flower's ghost. Growth is a death
on my youth laid.

We Love

about trees: past is never tall enough,
future too tall. Another spring will tell.

Tell another spring I will be there, and fairer.
I become myself, standing upon
that throat of swan
that striding giant I decree myself.

We love: in trees or men, how many die
forward on the blade.
I see men like forests
striding, like swans riding, royally, always
royally: though lowly afoot, striding into death.

What we love: there are not blades enough.

Tasks

Hercules strides back from hell, bearing
the starry fleece like a lamb at great breast:
Cerberus heels after: what a meek monster!

Whoever greets him, must attend: listen . . .
night is too short: moon declines to morning,
a ninth labor drones on sleepy children.

But Orpheus returns wearily among
shadows that waited him, waited to weep welcome
that beloved ghost his music could not quicken.

Why set man a task, why string his hands
delicately to five fingers, an ivory plectrum
against whose weal or bitter, hell is most proof?

Orpheus, remember Christ and the ninth hour:
his hands, empty of task or music, comprehend
what fled you in the dark arches. Here

blustering Hercules turns to water: his eyes
learn their first tears upon the dolorous dead.
Comfort there is none. But for compassion

the broken lyre stirs in your arms, like Phoenix.

Go Down on Knee

I saw an old wife stricken, the man
bending painfully above: let me serve, be
eyes, limbs.
                    Each wearing for better for
worse, the other's flesh, rent and patch: I do.
Bridal gown is yellow as bone, raveled

like youth out many a gay and slower
mile: stained bowler and waistcoat, a
rusty charmer.
                    Yet all days since, I see
visible things of this world, faultless
and heartening, go down on knee before, fashion
music toward, measure hope and
decline upon
                    the least audible heartbeat
of this holy darkness: I love you.

To a Pragmatist, in Death

Offer a flower
to hands that never bestowed or loved
one meek heraldic rose,
a secret spring he had merely to touch
and heart stood like a genie
in that dream he walked once only:
standing
to pluck a rose
he forgets even
why he desperately loved
and never bore
safely out of dream.
Well, a few lines
held to face like flowers, to breast like a heart

restore. Eternity is a rose
Dante says, he will wear, give: yes, have time for.

Chartres

Night to quiet countryside comes. The cathedral
casts from its sevenfold eye and altar
such look as even at sleeper's heart
is all a witness and scrutiny of love

such love is wings of the blackened stone giant
buttressed, chained to land a thousand years
which no searching plow ever turned, whose cruel prow
bears down on the tormented human surf

and whether land or seaside metaphor view it
cathedral is permanent and landlocked: but at evening
limbers stone wings for the tremendous passage,
mounts, bearing in talons an uprooted planet
despite, despite, into a Patmos morning.

Thirst

In him no beauty was
but body racked and robbed
and blood predicting darkly
no comeliness no wonder

against his pinioned arms
legion seas came marching
winds ran through his caved
breast and the sun was armored

in seamless womb on womb
unborn interminably
I started in his longing
and puffed his tongue to drought

in him no beauty was
no comeliness no wonder
who yet when he was lifted
had drawn all things to him

a fist to his face came sorrow
a thirst the thought of me

How Large

a lark must be
ears answer listening
but eyes closed, that otherwise
closed on lark like a brutish
hand, deceiving life
for sake of a size.

How large life is, stupid
years stutter over. Give me a hand
fast in mine, across sorrow
laid. My friend is Christ near.

Literal

is the wing's breadth that dares
more in age than in youth, unafraid of that height
where itself waits.
Literal the painter signs
continents he discovered he had
always inhabited: air is breathable,
streams are eyes, five days await
their naked crown.
Literal is every leaf
in the brown wood cloaking with mystery
the golden bough after whose literal glory
all things are made: do not be afraid
not to be me. Age and fierce thirst will never,
though eternity spring my root, admit me
into your height.
Literal a face from its easel
looks out: but no one looks quite in.
Alone among landscapes
you are signed: undiscovered.

A Voice of Leaves

Even to be a tree, erect and generous
to wear one's colors in and through,
leaf to heart, mild days to snow, is something:
the whole world cannot be men.
                                        Then make him worthy
the crown all things crowd forward
to place on him.
                                    I pray him that perfection
an oak stands for till it shatter under

time's fist he rides and turns lightly to air.

Late

I follow stumbling Jesus down the wall:
porter and brigand at his passing
swing wide his wounds and spread my hands for gold

then stand erect in her torrential glance
who flowers in the iron street
and gives me sudden spring to die in

nos morituri: he and I passed boyhood
both in country places, saw sunset finger
idly a first star, walked the enormous dawn

now tardy by centuries I come to town
only to see (as he) through fury
a woman standing though the skies are down.

This Book Bears

                                like a good voyager, marks of passage:
to proclaim, being loved
and led by hand through time, a life between lines.

Like a child's face: hold me to your face, see
the warm blood mount.
                                Like a hero: bathe me in some element
out of time: sentences spring their counterpoint,
man puts off his shadow, he is suddenly
alight.
                                Once, once on a time
victory beckoned, heel and profile,
spent runners on a vase.
                                                You exult? into your eyes
they pour, they prevail.

ABOUT THE AUTHOR

The complementary energies of teacher, priest, and poet are fused with compelling effect in the work of Father Daniel Berrigan.

The author of *Time Without Number* (Lamont Poetry Selection, 1957), which was called "literary magic" by Marianne Moore, and of *The Bride: Essays in The Church,* which *Sign Magazine* called "a Christian classic," Father Berrigan is a Professor of Dogmatic Theology at LeMoyne College in Syracuse, New York. His poems, essays, and reviews have appeared in *Saturday Review, Atlantic Monthly, Poetry, Thought, Commonweal,* and other magazines. In addition, he has lectured to many literary and university groups in this country and abroad.

Father Berrigan was born in Virginia, Minnesota, and has taught theology at Fordham University and done parish work in Brooklyn as well as in Paris. His encounters with the world and the city of men are altogether real; and in his poems about them he demonstrates the rightful credentials of intelligence and insight that define the authentic voice.